Rosary Novena

54 Day Rosary Novella

Intention:

Petition

J	S	G	J	S	G	J	S	G
J	S	G	J	S	G	J	S	G
J	S	G	J	S	G	J	S	G

Thanksgiving

J	S	G	J	S	G	J	S	G
J	S	G	J	S	G	J	S	G
J	S	G	J	S	G	J	S	G

Intention:

Petition

J	S	G	J	S	G	J	S	G
J	S	G	J	S	G	J	S	G
J	S	G	J	S	G	J	S	G

Thanksgiving

J	S	G	J	S	G	J	S	G
J	S	G	J	S	G	J	S	G
J	S	G	J	S	G	J	S	G

Table of Contents

Intention:

Petition

J	S	G	J	S	G	J	S	G
J	S	G	J	S	G	J	S	G
J	S	G	J	S	G	J	S	G

Thanksgiving

J	S	G	J	S	G	J	S	G
J	S	G	J	S	G	J	S	G
J	S	G	J	S	G	J	S	G

Intention:

Petition

J	S	G	J	S	G	J	S	G
J	S	G	J	S	G	J	S	G
J	S	G	J	S	G	J	S	G

Thanksgiving

J	S	G	J	S	G	J	S	G
J	S	G	J	S	G	J	S	G
J	S	G	J	S	G	J	S	G

Intention:

Petition

J	S	G	J	S	G	J	S	G
J	S	G	J	S	G	J	S	G
J	S	G	J	S	G	J	S	G

Thanksgiving

J	S	G	J	S	G	J	S	G
J	S	G	J	S	G	J	S	G
J	S	G	J	S	G	J	S	G

Origin and Method

This devotion, which the author has called the 'Rosary Novenas to Our Lady,' is of comparatively recent origin. In an apparition of Our Lady of Pompeii, which occurred in 1884 at Naples, in the house of Commander Agrelli, the heavenly Mother deigned to make known the manner in which she desires to be invoked.

For thirteen months Fortuna Agrelli, the daughter of the Commander, had endured dreadful sufferings and torturous cramps; she had been given up by the most celebrated physicians. On February 16, 1884, the afflicted girl and her relatives commenced a novena of Rosaries. The Queen of the Holy Rosary favored her with an apparition on March 3rd. Mary, sitting upon a high throne, surrounded by luminous figures, held the divine Child on her lap, and in her hand a Rosary. The Virgin Mother and the holy Infant were clad in goldembroidered garments. They were accompanied by St. Dominic and St. Catherine of Siena. The throne was profusely decorated with flowers; the beauty of Our Lady was marvelous.

Mary looked upon the sufferer with maternal tenderness, and the patient saluted her with the words: '*Queen of the Holy Rosary, be gracious to me; restore me to health! I have already prayed to thee in a novena, O Mary, but have not yet experienced thy aid. I am so anxious to be cured!*'

'*Child,*' responded the Blessed Virgin, *thou hast invoked me by various titles and hast always obtained favors from me. Now, since thou hast called me by that title so pleasing to me, 'Queen of the Holy Rosary,' I can no longer refuse the favor thou dost petition; for this name is most precious and dear to me. Make three novenas, and thou shalt obtain all.*'

Once more the Queen of the Holy Rosary appeared to her and said, '*Whoever desires to obtain favors from me should make three novenas of the prayers of the Rosary, and three novenas in thanksgiving.*'

"This miracle of the Rosary made a very deep impression on Pope Leo XIII, and greatly contributed to the fact that in so many circular letters he urged all Christians to love the Rosary and say it fervently."

The Novena consists of five decades of the Rosary each day for twenty seven days in petition; then immediately five decades each day for twenty seven days in thanksgiving, whether or not the request has been granted.

The meditations vary from day to day. On the first day meditate on the Joyful Mysteries: on the second day the Sorrowful Mysteries: on the third day the Glorious Mysteries: on the fourth day meditate again on the Joyful Mysteries; and so on throughout the fifty four days.

A laborious Novena, but a *Novena of Love*. You who are sincere will not find it too difficult, *if you really wish to obtain your request*. Should you not obtain the favor you seek, be assured that the Rosary Queen, who knows what each one stands most in need of, has heard your prayer. You will not have prayed in vain. No prayer ever went unheard. And Our Blessed Lady has never been known to fail.

Look upon each Hail Mary as a rare and beautiful rose which you lay at Mary's feet. These spiritual roses, bound in a wreath with Spiritual Communions, will be a most pleasing and acceptable gift to her, and will bring down upon you special graces.

If you would reach the innermost recesses of her heart, lavishly bedeck your wreath with spiritual diamonds holy communions. Then her joy will be unbounded, and she will open wide the channel of her choicest graces to you.

54 Day Rosary Novena Prayers

The Joyful Mysteries

Prayer before the recitation: Sign of the cross. Hail Mary.

In petition: Hail, Queen of the Most Holy Rosary, my Mother Mary, hail! At thy feet I humbly kneel to offer thee a Crown of Roses snow white buds to remind thee of thy joys each bud recalling to thee a holy mystery; each ten bound together with my petition for a particular grace. O Holy Queen, dispenser of God's graces, and Mother of all who invoke thee! thou canst not look upon my gift and fail to see its binding. As thou receivest my gift, so wilt thou receive my petition; from thy bounty thou wilt give me the favor I so earnestly and trustingly seek. I despair of nothing that I ask of thee. Show thyself my Mother!

In thanksgiving: Hail, Queen of the Most Holy Rosary, my Mother Mary, hail! At thy feet I gratefully kneel to offer thee a Crown of Roses snow white buds to remind thee of thy joys each bud recalling to thee a holy mystery; each ten bound together with my petition for a particular grace. O Holy Queen, Dispenser of God's graces. and Mother of all who invoke thee! thou canst not look upon my gift and fail to see its binding. As thou receivest my gift, so wilt thou receive my thanksgiving; from thy bounty thou hast given me the favor I so earnestly and trustingly sought. I despaired not of what I asked of thee, and thou hast truly shown thyself my Mother.

- Creed, Our Father, 3 Hail Marys, Glory be to the Father.

The Annunciation

Sweet Mother Mary, meditating on the Mystery of the Annunciation, when the angel Gabriel appeared to thee with the tidings that thou wert to become the Mother of God; greeting thee with that sublime salutation, *"Hail, full of grace! the Lord is with thee!"* and thou didst humbly submit thyself to the will of the Father, responding: *"Behold the handmaid of the Lord. Be it done unto me according to thy word."*

I humbly pray: Our Father, 10 Hail Marys, Glory be to the Father.

I bind these snow white buds with a petition for the virtue of **Humility** and humbly lay this bouquet at thy feet.

The Visitation

Sweet Mother Mary, meditating on the Mystery of the Visitation, when, upon thy visit to thy holy cousin, Elizabeth, she greeted thee with the prophetic utterance, *"Blessed art thou among women, and blessed is the fruit of thy womb!"* and thou didst answer with that canticle of canticles, the Magnificat.

I humbly pray: Our Father, 10 Hail Marys, Glory be to the Father.

I bind these snow white buds with a petition for the virtue of **Charity** and humbly lay this bouquet at thy feet.

The Nativity

Sweet Mother Mary, meditating on the Mystery of the Nativity of Our Lord, when, thy time being completed, thou didst bring forth, O holy Virgin, the Redeemer of the world in a stable at Bethlehem; whereupon choirs of angels filled the heavens with their exultant song of praise *"Glory to God in the highest, and on earth peace to men of good will."*

I humbly pray: Our Father, 10 Hail Marys, Glory be to the Father.

I bind these snow white buds with a petition for the virtue of **Detachment from the world** and humbly lay this bouquet at thy feet.

The Presentation

Sweet Mother Mary, meditating on the Mystery of the Presentation, when, in obedience to the Law of Moses, thou didst present thy Child in the Temple, where the holy prophet Simeon, taking the Child in his arms, offered thanks to God for sparing him to look upon his Saviour and foretold thy sufferings by the words: "*Thy soul also a sword shall pierce . . .*"

I humbly pray: Our Father, 10 Hail Marys, Glory be to the Father.

I bind these snowwhite buds with a petition for the virtue of **Purity** and humbly lay this bouquet at thy feet.

The Finding Of The Child Jesus In The Temple

Sweet Mother Mary, meditating on the Mystery of the Finding of the Child Jesus in the Temple, when, having sought Him for three days, sorrowing, thy heart was gladdened upon finding Him in the Temple speaking to the doctors; and when, upon thy request, He obediently returned home with thee.

I humbly pray:

Our Father, 10 Hail Marys, Glory be to the Father.

I bind these snow white buds with a petition for the virtue of **Obedience to the will of God** and humbly lay this bouquet at thy feet.

Spiritual Communion:

MY JESUS, really present in the most holy Sacrament of the Altar, since I cannot now receive Thee under the sacramental veil, I beseech Thee, with a heart full of love and longing, to come spiritually into my soul through the immaculate heart of Thy most holy Mother, and abide with me forever.

Thou in me,
And I in Thee,
In Time and in
Eternity, In Mary.

In petition: Sweet Mother Mary, I offer thee this Spiritual Communion to bind my bouquets in a wreath to place upon thy brow. O my Mother! look with favor upon my gift, and in thy love obtain for me _____Hail, Mary, etc.

In thanksgiving: Sweet Mother Mary, I offer thee this Spiritual Communion to bind my bouquets in a wreath to place upon thy brow in thanksgiving for _____which thou in thy love hast obtained for me. Hail, Mary, etc.

Prayer

O God! Whose only begotten Son, by His life, death, and resurrection, has purchased for us the reward of eternal life; grant, we beseech Thee, that, meditating upon these mysteries of the Most Holy Rosary of the Blessed Virgin Mary, we may imitate what they contain and obtain what they promise. Through the same Christ our Lord. Amen.

May the divine assistance remain always with us. And may the souls of the faithful departed, through the mercy of God, rest in peace. Amen. Holy Virgin, with thy loving Child, thy blessing give to us this day (night). In the name of the Father, and of the Son, and of the Holy Ghost. Amen.

The Sorrowful Mysteries

Prayer before the recitation: Sign of the cross. Hail Mary.

In petition: Hail, Queen of the Most Holy Rosary, my Mother Mary, hail! At thy feet I humbly kneel to offer thee a Crown of Roses blood red roses to remind thee of the passion of thy divine Son, with Whom thou didst so fully partake of its bitterness each rose recalling to thee a holy mystery; each ten bound together with my petition for a particular grace. O Holy Queen, dispenser of God's graces, and Mother of all who invoke thee! Thou canst not look upon my gift and fail to see its binding. As thou receivest my gift, so wilt thou receive my petition; from thy bounty thou wilt give me the favor I so earnestly and trustingly seek. I despair of nothing that I ask of thee. Show thyself my Mother!

In thanksgiving: Hail, Queen of the Most Holy Rosary, my Mother Mary, hail! At thy feet I gratefully kneel to offer thee a Crown of Roses blood red roses to remind thee of the passion of thy divine Son, with Whom thou didst so fully partake of its bitterness each rose recalling to thee a holy mystery; each ten bound together with my petition for a particular grace. O Holy Queen, dispenser of God's graces, and Mother of all who invoke thee! Thou canst not look upon my gift and fail to see its binding. As thou receivest my gift, so wilt thou receive my thanksgiving; from thy bounty thou hast given me the favor I so earnestly and trustingly sought. I despaired not of what I asked of thee, and thou hast truly shown thyself my Mother.

●   Creed, Our Father, 3 Hail Marys, Glory be to the Father.

The Agony

O most sorrowful Mother Mary, meditating on the Mystery of the Agony of Our Lord in the Garden, when, in the grotto of the Garden of Olives, Jesus saw the sins of the world unfolded before Him by Satan, who sought to dissuade Him from the sacrifice He was about to make; when, His soul shrinking from the sight, and His precious blood flowing from every pore at the vision of the torture and death He was to undergo, thy own sufferings, dear Mother, the future sufferings of His Church, and His own sufferings in the Blessed Sacrament, He cried in anguish, "*Abba! Father! if it be possible, let this chalice pass from Me*"; but, immediately resigning Himself to His Father's will, He prayed, "*Not as I will, but as Thou wilt!*"

I humbly pray: Our Father, 10 Hail Marys, Glory be to the Father.

I bind these blood red roses with a petition for the virtue of **Resignation to the will of God** and humbly lay this bouquet at thy feet.

The Scourging

O most sorrowful Mother Mary, meditating on the Mystery of the Scourging of Our Lord, when, at Pilate's command, thy divine Son, stripped of His garments and bound to a pillar, was lacerated from head to foot with cruel scourges and His flesh torn away until His mortified body could bear no more.

I humbly pray: Our Father, 10 Hail Marys, Glory be to the Father.

I bind these blood red roses with a petition for the virtue of **Mortification** and humbly lay this bouquet at thy feet.

The Crowning With Thorns

O most sorrowful Mother Mary, meditating on the Mystery of the Crowning of Our Lord with thorns, when, the soldiers, binding about His head a crown of sharp thorns, showered blows upon it, driving the thorns deeply into His head; then, in mock adoration, knelt before Him, crying, "*Hail, King of the Jews!*"

I humbly pray: Our Father, 10 Hail Marys, Glory be to the Father.

I bind these bloodred roses with a petition for the virtue of **Humility** and humbly lay this bouquet at thy feet.

The Carrying Of The Cross

O most sorrowful Mother Mary, meditating on the Mystery of the Carrying of the Cross, when, with the heavy wood of the cross upon His shoulders, thy divine Son was dragged, weak and suffering, yet patient, through the streets, amidst the revilements of the people, to Calvary; falling often, but urged along by the cruel blows of His executioners.

I humbly pray: Our Father, 10 Hail Marys, Glory be to the Father.

I bind these bloodred roses with a petition for the virtue of **Patience in Adversity** and humbly lay this bouquet at thy feet.

The Crucifixion

O most sorrowful Mother Mary, meditating on the Mystery of the Crucifixion, when, having been stripped of His garments, thy divine Son was nailed to the cross, upon which He died after three hours of indescribable agony, during which time He begged from His Father forgiveness for His enemies.

I humbly pray: Our Father, 10 Hail Marys, Glory be to the Father.

I bind these bloodred roses with a petition for the virtue of **Love of our enemies** and humbly lay this bouquet at thy feet.

Spiritual Communion

MY JESUS, really present in the most holy Sacrament of the Altar, since I cannot now receive Thee under the sacramental veil, I beseech Thee, with a heart full of love and longing, to come spiritually into my soul through the immaculate heart of Thy most holy Mother, and abide with me forever.

Thou in me,
And I in Thee,
In Time and in
Eternity, In Mary.

In petition: Sweet Mother Mary, I offer thee this Spiritual Communion to bind my bouquets in a wreath to place upon thy brow. O my Mother! look with favor upon my gift, and in thy love obtain for me _____Hail, Mary, etc.

In thanksgiving: Sweet Mother Mary, I offer thee this Spiritual Communion to bind my bouquets in a wreath to place upon thy brow in thanksgiving for _____which thou in thy love hast obtained for me. Hail, Mary, etc.

Prayer

O God! Whose only begotten Son, by His life, death, and resurrection, has purchased for us the reward of eternal life; grant, we beseech Thee, that, meditating upon these mysteries of the Most Holy Rosary of the Blessed Virgin Mary, we may imitate what they contain and obtain what they promise. Through the same Christ our Lord. Amen.

May the divine assistance remain always with us. And may the souls of the faithful departed, through the mercy of God, rest in peace. Amen. Holy Virgin, with thy loving Child, thy blessing give to us this day (night). In the name of the Father, and of the Son, and of the Holy Ghost. Amen.

The Glorious Mysteries

Prayer before the recitation: Sign of the cross. Hail Mary.

In petition: Hail, Queen of the Most Holy Rosary, my Mother Mary, hail! At thy feet I humbly kneel to offer thee a Crown of Roses full blown white roses, tinged with the red of the passion, to remind thee of thy glories, fruits of the sufferings of thy Son and thee each rose recalling to thee a holy mystery; each ten bound together with my petition for a particular grace. O Holy Queen, dispenser of God's graces, and Mother of all who invoke thee! Thou canst not look upon my gift and fail to see its binding. As thou receivest my gift, so wilt thou receive my petition; from thy bounty thou wilt give me the favor I so earnestly and trustingly seek. I despair of nothing that I ask of thee. Show thyself my Mother!

In thanksgiving: Hail!, Queen of the Most Holy Rosary, my Mother Mary, hail! At thy feet I gratefully kneel to offer thee a Crown of Roses full blown white roses, tinged with the red of the passion, to remind thee of thy glories, fruits of the sufferings of thy Son and thee each rose recalling to thee a holy mystery; each ten bound together with my petition for a particular grace. O Holy Queen, dispenser of God's graces, and Mother of all who invoke thee! thou canst not look upon my gift and fail to see its binding. As thou receivest my gift, so wilt thou receive my thanksgiving; from thy bounty thou hast given me the favor I so earnestly and trustingly sought. I despaired not of what I asked of thee, and thou hast truly shown thyself my Mother.

- Creed, Our Father, 3 Hail Marys, Glory be to the Father.

The Resurrection

O glorious Mother Mary, meditating on the Mystery of the Resurrection of Our Lord from the Dead, when, on the morning of the third day after His death and burial. He arose from the dead and appeared to thee, dear Mother, and filled thy heart with unspeakable joy; then appeared to the holy women, and to His disciples, who adored Him as their risen God.

I humbly pray: Our Father, 10 Hail Marys, Glory be to the Father.

I bind these full blown roses with a petition for the virtue of **Faith** and humbly lay this bouquet at thy feet.

The Ascension

O glorious Mother Mary, meditating on the Mystery of the Ascension, when thy divine Son, after forty days on earth, went to Mount Olivet accompanied by His disciples and thee, where all adored Him for the last time, after which He promised to remain with them until the end of the world; then, extending His pierced hands over all in a last blessing, He ascended before their eyes into heaven.

I humbly pray: Our Father, 10 Hail Marys, Glory be to the Father.

I bind these full blown roses with a petition for the virtue of **Hope** and humbly lay this bouquet at thy feet.

The Descent of the Holy Ghost

O glorious Mother Mary, meditating on the Mystery of the Descent of the Holy Ghost, when, the apostles being assembled with thee in a house in Jerusalem, the Holy Ghost descended upon them in the form of fiery tongues, inflaming the hearts of the apostles with the fire of divine love, teaching them all truths, giving to them the gift of tongues, and filling thee with the plenitude of His grace, inspired thee to pray for the apostles and the first Christians.

I humbly pray: Our Father, 10 Hail Marys, Glory be to the Father.

I bind these fullblown roses with a petition for the virtue of **Charity** and humbly lay this bouquet at thy feet.

The Assumption Of Our Blessed Mother Into Heaven

O glorious Mother Mary, meditating on the Mystery of Thy Assumption into Heaven, when, consumed with the desire to be united with thy divine Son in heaven, thy soul departed from thy body and united itself to Him, Who, out of the excessive love He bore for thee, His Mother, whose virginal body was His first tabernacle, took that body into heaven and there, amidst the acclaims of the angels and saints, reinfused into it thy soul.

I humbly pray: Our Father, 10 Hail Marys, Glory be to the Father.

I bind these fullblown roses with a petition for the virtue of **Union with Christ** and humbly lay this bouquet at thy feet.

The Coronation Of Our Blessed Mother In Heaven As Its Queen

O glorious Mother Mary, meditating on the Mystery of Thy Coronation in Heaven, when, upon being taken up to heaven after thy death, thou wert triply crowned as the august Queen of Heaven by God the Father as His beloved Daughter, by God the Son as His dearest Mother, and by God the Holy Ghost as His chosen Spouse; the most perfect adorer of the Blessed Trinity, pleading our cause as our most powerful and merciful Mother, through thee.

I humbly pray: Our Father, 10 Hail Marys, Glory be to the Father.

I bind these full blown roses with a petition for the virtue of **Union with thee** and humbly lay this bouquet at thy feet.

Spiritual Communion

MY JESUS, really present in the most holy Sacrament of the Altar, since I cannot now receive Thee under the sacramental veil, I beseech Thee, with a heart full of love and longing, to come spiritually into my soul through the immaculate heart of Thy most holy Mother, and abide with me forever.

Thou in me,
And I in Thee,
In Time and in
Eternity, In Mary.

In petition: Sweet Mother Mary, I offer thee this Spiritual Communion to bind my bouquets in a wreath to place upon thy brow. O my Mother! look with favor upon my gift, and in thy love obtain for me _____Hail, Mary, etc.

In thanksgiving: Sweet Mother Mary, I offer thee this Spiritual Communion to bind my bouquets in a wreath to place upon thy brow in thanksgiving for _____which thou in thy love hast obtained for me. Hail, Mary, etc.

Prayer

O God! Whose only begotten Son, by His life, death, and resurrection, has purchased for us the reward of eternal life; grant, we beseech Thee, that, meditating upon these mysteries of the Most Holy Rosary of the Blessed Virgin Mary, we may imitate what they contain and obtain what they promise. Through the same Christ our Lord. Amen.

May the divine assistance remain always with us. And may the souls of the faithful departed, through the mercy of God, rest in peace. Amen. Holy Virgin, with thy loving Child, thy blessing give to us this day (night). In the name of the Father, and of the Son, and of the Holy Ghost. Amen.

How to Make A Novena

From <u>Prayer: Its necessity Its power Its conditions</u> By Rev. Ferreol Girardy, C.Ss.R., 1916

Fourthly, making a Novena is also an efficacious means of obtaining graces and favors from God. A Novena is a nine days' prayer or supplication. A Novena is generally made thus: A certain prayer or certain prayers for a certain specified object are said for nine consecutive days and, after a good confession, holy Communion is received on the tenth day. What prayer or prayers we should say are left to our choice; for instance, we may recite daily nine Hail Marys, or a decade or five decades of the rosary, a litany, hear holy Mass, make a visit to the Blessed Sacrament, etc. To the prayers we recite we may join a certain alms, a certain act of self-denial, or some other good work, according to our devotion or to the circumstances in which we are placed. But our prayers, our good works should be performed with earnestness and fervor. Our Novena will be still more efficacious, if we have the Sacrifice of the Mass offered for our intention once or oftener during the Novena. If in our power, it would be well, if we would request others, especially good and pious souls, to join us in our Novena. Novenas may be made, for instance, in honor of or to the Sacred Heart of Jesus, in honor of the Blessed Virgin, of Our Lady of Mercy, of Good Counsel, of Lourdes, of Perpetual Help, to Mary Refuge of sinners, in honor of St. Joseph, St. Gerard Majella, etc. Prayers and Novenas may be addressed privately to persons who have died in the odor of sanctity, especially if the Cause or Process of their Beatification has already been introduced, as for instance, Sister Thérèse of the Infant Jesus and the Holy Face. The reason is that God, when He wants to have persons honored as saints by the Church, grants to that end many wonderful favors and even miracles to prove their sanctity. A Novena may be made for the benefit of the souls in purgatory to obtain a grace or favor through their intercession. Moreover, they who make a Novena for a certain grace, usually promise to God some prayer or good work as a thanksgiving, if their prayer is granted. For instance, if their prayer is granted they will hear Mass daily, or every Saturday for a year or more, or will go weekly to confession and holy Communion, or abstain from certain delicacies or beverages for a stated time, or from certain comforts or amusements, or perform certain penances, etc.

Beware of promising too much, or of undertaking certain rigorous penances without your confessor's special permission. And if your prayers have been granted, show your gratitude to God by thanking Him from your inmost heart, and faithfully performing your promises. If your prayers have not been heard in the manner you desired, do not murmur or complain, but be resigned to God's holy will, and feel confident that He has given or will give you something else more necessary or useful to you, for never is a true and sincere prayer lost.

Prayer of Saint John Eudes to Admirable Heart of Mary for Conversions

Hail Mary, Daughter of God the Father.
Hail Mary, Mother of God the Son.
Hail Mary, Spouse of the Holy Ghost.
Hail Mary, Temple of the Divinity.
Hail Mary, Immaculate lily of the resplendent and ever-peaceful Trinity. Hail Mary, Radiant rose of heavenly fragrance.
Hail Mary, Virgin of virgins, virgin most faithful, of whom the King of Heaven did will to be born.
Hail Mary, Queen of martyrs, whose soul was pierced with a sword of sorrow.
Hail Mary, Queen of the universe, to whom all power has been given in heaven and on earth.
Hail Mary, Queen of my heart, my mother, my life, my consolation, and my dearest hope.
Hail Mary, Mother most amiable.
Hail Mary, Mother most admirable.
Hail Mary, Mother of Mercy.
Hail Mary, full of grace, the Lord is with thee.
Blessed art thou amongst women.
And blessed is the fruit of thy womb, Jesus.
And blessed be thy spouse, St. Joseph.
And blessed be thy father, St. Joachim.
And blessed be thy mother, St. Anne.
And blessed be thy adopted son, St. John.
And blessed be thy angel, St. Gabriel.
And blessed be the Eternal Father who chose thee.

Fasting on Saturday

Sermons of Saint Alphonsus, for the Second Lord's Day after Epiphany: "But, to obtain special favors in her honor certain devotions practiced by her servants; such as, first, to recite every day at least five decades of the Rosary; secondly, to fast every Saturday in her honor. Many persons fast every Saturday on bread and water: you should fast in this manner at least on the vigils of her seven principle festivals."

From Glories of Mary

MANY servants of Mary, on Saturdays and the vigils of her feast, are accustomed to honor her by fasting on bread and water. It is well known that Saturday is a day dedicated by the holy Church to the honor of the Virgin, because on this day, says St. Bernard, she remained constant in the faith after the death of her Son.

For this reason the servants of Mary never fail on this day to offer her some special homage; and particularly the fast on bread and water, as St. Charles Borromeo, Cardinal Toledo, and so many others practised it. Rittard, Bishop of Bamberg, and Father Joseph Arriaga, of the Society of Jesus, did not even taste food on Saturday. The great graces which the mother of God afterwards bestowed upon those who practised this devotion, may be read in the writings of Father Auriemma. It is sufficient for us to mention the compassion which she showed to that bandit chief, who on account of this devotion, was permitted to remain alive, although his head had been cut off, and although he was under the displeasure of God, and was enabled to make his confession before dying. He afterwards declared that the holy virgin, for this fasting which he had offered her, had preserved him in life, and he then suddenly expired. It would not then be a very extraordinary thing, if any one, especially devoted to Mary, and particularly if he had already deserved hell, should offer to her this fast on Saturday. He who practises this devotion, I may say, will hardly be condemned; not that our Lady will deliver him by a miracle if he dies in mortal sin, as happened to the bandit; such prodigies of divine mercy seldom take place, and it would be madness to expect eternal salvation by them. But I do say that the divine mother will readily obtain perseverance and divine grace and a good death for him who will practise this devotion. All the brothers of our little congregation who can do so, fast on bread and water on Saturday, in honor of Mary. I say those who can do so, meaning, that if any one is prevented from doing so on account of ill health, at least on Saturday, he may content himself with one dish, make a common fast, or at least abstain from fruits or other agreeable food. It is necessary on Saturday to offer special devotions to our Lady, to receive communion, or, at least, hear Mass, visit some image of the Virgin, wear hair-cloth, and the like. And at least on the vigils of the seven feasts of Mary, let her servants endeavor to offer this fasting on bread, or in any other manner they are able.

First Saturdays

Jesus appeared to Sister Lucy on December 10, 1925 to ask for the devotion of First Saturdays: "Behold, my daughter, my Heart surrounded with the thorns with which ungrateful men continually pierce it by their blasphemies (heresies?) and ingratitudes. Do you at least try to console me, and for my part I declare to you that I promise to assist at the hour of death with the graces necessary for salvation all those who on the first Saturday of five consecutive months shall go to confession, receive Holy Communion, say five decades of the rosary and keep me company during a quarter of an hour, meditating on the mysteries of the rosary with the intention of offering reparation to me."

Our Lady of Pfaffenhofen (1946): "Observe the Holy Saturday devoted to me the way I have suggested it. The apostles and priests ought to devote themselves to Me especially in order that the great sacrifices which the Inscrutable One demands from them very particularly may grow in holiness and worthiness when they are laid into My hands. Make many sacrifices for Me and make your prayer a sacrifice. Be selfless." "I am the great Mediatrix of Grace. The Father wants the world to recognize His Handmaid. Men must believe that I am the eternal Bride of the Holy Ghost, the faithful Mediatrix of all graces. My sign is about to appear. Thus God wills it. Only My children will recognize it because it manifests itself in hiding, and therefore they honor the Eternal One. I cannot reveal My power to the world as yet. I must go into retirement with My children. In hiding I will perform miracles in the souls until the (ordained?) number of victims is complete. It is up to you to shorten the days of darkness. Your prayers and sacrifices will destroy the image of the Beast."

The First Saturday consists of four parts. The first is the recitation of the Rosary, the second is Holy Communion. The third is Confession and the Final part is an additional fifteen minutes meditation on the mysteries of the Rosary. This should be continued for five months, although it is advisable to continue this the rest of our lives. We should add to this the Saturday fast at least on first Saturdays. For those who cannot communicate, a Solemn Spiritual Communion should be made and to replace the Confession a Perfect Act of Contrition made.

Scapular

From <u>The Glories of Mary</u> by Saint Alphonsus Ligouri

I will greatly rejoice in the Lord, and my soul shall be joyful in my God; for he hath clothed me with the garments of salvation; and with a robe of justice he hath covered me. Isaias 61, 10.

The Origin of This Devotion

The institution of the Scapular is to be attributed to St. Simon Stock, an Englishman by birth, one of the ornaments of the church in the thirteenth age.

Having retired to the desert at the age of twelve years, he passed thirty days in the practice of the most austere penance and contemplation. Meeting with some Carmelite religious, called brothers of the Virgin, on account of their tender devotion towards her, he took their habit, and went to pass six years of profound solitude on Mount Carmel. On his return to Europe, having become General of his order, in 1245, as he was one day asking the blessed Mother of God, in the simplicity of his confidence, to grant him a mark of her protection; she appeared to him in great glory, surrounded by myriads of angels. and holding in her hand a Scapular, or covering for the shoulders, Which she gave to him, saying these words: "My well beloved son, receive this Scapular which I present to you and to all the members of your order; it is by this sign that I wish you should be hereafter recognized as my children; it is a privilege granted you and all the children of Mount Carmel, so that whoever shall die invested with this holy habit shall have an assurance of my protection in escaping everlasting flames: "In quo quis moriens aeternum non patietur incendium:" it is a mark of predestination, a safeguard in dangers, an emblem of peace, and the symbol of perpetual alliance. This vision has been so well attested by all the evidences that could guaranty its authencity, that the wise Pope Benedict XIV, has not hesitated to say: "We believe it true and we are of opinion that all the world should hold it as true; hone visionem veram credimus, veramque habendam ab omnibus arbitramur. (De, Beat, 1V.--2. 9. et de Fest. II.-9.)" We will not then be astonished that this devotion has been rapidly propagated, and that it continues to flourish through out the catholic world.

Of the Advantages Which It Procures

It entitles us to the promises of the Blessed Virgin, that is to say that the Scapular: 1. Serves as a pledge of a more intimate and lasting union with the august queen of heaven; 2. It protects us, as a celestial armour, in the dangers both of soul and body; 3. It becomes for us a preservative against the flames of hell, by assuring to us, during life and at the hour of death, the most special aid of the powerful Mother of God. We can undoubtedly be saved without wearing the Scapular, but with it salvation is easier and more certain; what more is necessary to attach us to it?

II We participate in all the good works of the Carmelite order, as is expressed in the formula of the reception: the first says In virtue of the power which has been intrusted to me, I receive and admit you to the full participation of all the prayers, penances, suffrages, alms, watchings, masses, offices and other spiritual duties, which are performed day and night, in every part of the world, through the mercy of Jesus Christ, by all the religious of the holy order of Mount Carmel.

We Gain Numbers Indulgences
Plenary Indulgences

1. On the day of our reception. (Paul V.)

2. On the Feast of our Lady of Mount Carmel, the 16th of July, or on one of the days of the Octave. (Paul III. Benedict.)

3. On the day of each month when there is a procession in honour of the blessed Virgin, when we assist at it. (Paul V.)

4. At the article of death, provided we pronounce at least with the heart, the holy name of Jesus.

5. Any time that the other confraternities enjoy any plenary indulgence. (Sixtus IV.—Clement VIII.)

Partial Indulgences

1. An indulgence of 5 years and 5 quarantines to members who accompany the holy Viaticum, and pray for the sick.

2. Of 5 years and 5 quarantines to all those who communicate once a month, and pray according to the intentions of our holy father, the Pope.

3. Of 100 days every time we perform a spiritual or corporal work of mercy.

4. Of 40 days, when we recite each day 7 Paters and Aves, etc.—all these different indulgences are applicable to the souls in Purgatory.

Sabbatine Privilege

Note.—A term derived from the Jewish Sabbath, our Saturday.

"It is not only in this life," says the Roman Breviary, "the B. V. Mary shows herself favourable, to the children of Mount Carmel, it is also in the life to come; for her power and her goodness extend every where. All those who wear the Scapular are careful to recite the few prayers prescribed, and preserve chastity according to their state of life, may hope (pie creditur,) that should they have to suffer the fire of purgatory, Mary will come to console them in her maternal tenderness, and cause them to enter their heavenly country as soon as possible; (quantocius,) especially on Saturday, the day consecrated to her, adds Pope Paul V in a bull of 1612.

When a true Christian is at the point of death, with what earnestness does he not recommend himself to his parents and friends, that they may abridge by their prayers the time of expiation which he dreads! But will they be faithful to this injunction? Will they pray for him? Will they procure for him the prayers of others? He knows not, and has too often reason to doubt it; men so soon forget! The servant of Mary has no such fears—he has only to observe some easy practices to be sure of relief; for Mary does not forget, as men do! She remembers her children, she remembers also her promises; and soon introduced into glory, they feel the happiness of having been faithful to her.

The Duties to be Fulfilled

The devotion of the Scapular imposes no obligation under pain of sin; but the privileges which it grants are not obtained but on certain conditions.

1. In order to be entitled to a more special protection of the B. V. M., the merits of the Carmelites, and the plenary and partial indulgences, three things are necessary: 1. To be received by a priest duly authorized; 2. To wear the Scapular constantly; 3 To be inscribed upon the register of the confraternity.

2. To obtain the Sabbatine indulgence, chastity must be observed according to each ones state, and the little office of the blessed Virgin or the canonical office recited. The office may be supplied by the fasts of the church and abstinence on Wednesday and Saturday; or if these fasts and abstinences are not possible, by some works equally painful and meritorious, as prescribed by a priest authorized to receive members, or by the confessor. Any one neglecting to gain the Sabbatine indulgence, does not lose the benefit of the other privileges.

In order to gain any plenary indulgence, confession, communion, and prayer, according to the intentions of the church (i.e. the Pope), are requisite.

Visits to the Blessed Virgin Mary

From Saint Alphonsus, <u>The Holy Eucharist</u>:

And now as to the visits to the Most Blessed Virgin, the opinion of St. Bernard is well known, and generally believed: it is, that God dispenses no graces otherwise than through the hands of Mary: 'God wills that we should receive nothing that does not pass through Mary's hands.' Hence Father Suarez declares that it is now the sentiment of the universal Church, that 'the intercession of Mary is not only useful, but even necessary to obtain graces.' And we may remark that the Church gives us strong grounds for this belief, by applying the words of Sacred Scripture to Mary, and make her say: 'In me is all hope of life and virtue. Come over to me, all ye that desire.' Let all come to me; for I am the hope of all that you can desire. Hence she then adds: 'Blessed is the man that heareth me, and that watcheth daily at my gates, and waiteth at the posts of my doors.' Blessed is he who is diligent in coming every day to the door of my powerful intercession; for by finding me he will find life and eternal salvation: 'He that shall find me he will find life, and shall have salvation from the Lord.' Hence it is not without reason that the Holy Church wills that we should all call her our common hope, by saluting her saying, 'Hail, our hope!'

'Let us then,' says St. Bernard (who went so far as to call Mary 'the whole ground of his hope'), 'seek for graces, and seek them through Mary.' Otherwise, says St. Anotninus, if we ask for graces without her intercession, we shall be making an effort to fly without wings, and we shall obtain nothing: 'He who asks without her as his guide, attempted to fly without wings.'

In Father Autiemma's little book, <u>Affetti Scambievoli</u>, we read of innumerable favors granted by the Mother of God to those who practised this most profitable devotion of often visiting her in her churches or before some image. We read of the graces which she granted in these visits to Saint Albert the Great, to the Abbot Rupert, to Father Suarez, especially when she obtained for them the gift of understanding, by which they afterwards became so renowned throughout the Church for their great learning: the graces which she granted to Saint John Berchmans of the Society of Jesus, who was in the daily habit of visiting Mary in a chapel of the Roman college; he declared that he renounced all earthly love, to love no other after God than the Most Blessed Virgin, and had written at the foot of the image of his believed Lady: 'I will never rest until I shall have obtained a tender love for my Mother;' the graces which she granted to Saint Bernadine of Sienna, who in his youth also went every day to visit her in a chapel near the city-gate, and declared that the Lady had ravished his heart. Hence he called her his beloved, and said that he could not do less than often visit her; and by her means he afterwards obtained the grace to renounce the world, and to become what he afterwards was, a great saint and the apostle of Italy.

Do you, then, be also careful always to join to your daily visit to the Most Blessed Sacrament a visit to the most holy Virgin May in some church, or at least before a devout image of her in your own house. If you do this with tender affection and confidence, you may hope to receive great things from this most gracious Lady, who, as St. Andrew of Crete says, always bestows great gifts on those who offer her even the least act of homage.

The Franciscan Crown

Seven decades of One Our Father and Ten Hail Marys:

The Annunciation

The Visitation

The Birth of Our Lord

The Adoration of the Magi

The Finding of the Child Jesus in the Temple

The Resurrection of Our Lord

The Assumption of the Blessed Virgin Mary

Follow with two Hail Marys in honor of the 72 years of the Blessed Virgin Mary's life.

Follow this with one Our Father and one Hail Mary for the intentions of the Holy Father.

The intentions of the Supreme Pontiff are: the exaltation of Holy Mother Church, the extirpation (overcoming) of heresies, propagation of the Faith, the conversion of sinners and peace among Christian nations. Unless specific prayers are prescribed for the Pope's intentions, any vocal prayers may be used.

The Franciscan Crown also called the Rosary of the Seven Joys of the Blessed Virgin, dated back to the year 1422. The famous Franciscan historian, Fr. Luke Wadding, relates that a very pious young man, who had been admitted to the Franciscan Order in that year, had, previous to his reception, been accustomed to adorn a statue of the Blessed Virgin with a wreath of beautiful flowers as a mark of his piety and devotion. Not being able to continue this practice in the novitiate, he repined very much, and finally decided to quit the cloister and return to the world.

Our Lady then appeared to him and prevented him from carrying out his purpose. "Do not be sad and cast down, my son." She said sweetly, "because you are no longer permitted to place a wreath of flowers on my statue.

"I shall teach you to change this pious practice into one that will be far more pleasing to me and far more meritorious to your soul. In place of the flowers, you can weave for me a crown from the flowers of your prayers that will always remain fresh and can always be had.

"Recite one Our Father and ten Hail Marys in honor of the joy I experienced when the angel announced to me the Incarnation of the Son of God. Repeat these same prayers in honor of the joy I felt on visiting my cousin Elizabeth. Say them again in honor of the supreme happiness that filled my heart on giving birth to Christ the Savior, without pain and without the loss of my virginity. Recite the same prayers a fourth time in honor of the joy I felt when presenting my Divine Son to the adoration of the Magi. Repeat them for the fifth time in honor of the joy that thrilled my soul when, after seeking Jesus with deep sorrow for three days, I found Him at last among the doctors in the Temple. Sixthly, recite one Our Father and then ten Hail Marys in honor of the joy I experienced on beholding my Divine Son gloriously risen from the grave on Easter Sunday. Finally, for the seventh time, repeat these prayers in honor of my own most glorious and joyful Assumption into heaven, when I was crowned Queen of heaven and earth. If you recite these prayers as I have directed, rest assured, dear son, you will weave a crown for me a most beautiful and acceptable crown and will merit for yourself innumerable graces."

When Our Lady had disappeared, the overjoyed novice at once began to recite the prayers in honor of her Seven Joys, as she had directed. While he was deeply engrossed in this devotion, the novice master happened to pass by and, behold, he say an angel weaving a marvelous wreath of roses and after every tenth rose he inserted a golden lily. When the wreath was finished, the angel placed it on the head of the praying novice. The master then demanded under holy obedience that the youth tell him the meaning of this vision. Joyfully, yet fearfully, the novice complied. The good priest was so impressed with what he had seen and heard, that he immediately made it known to his brethren. Thus the practice of reciting the Crown of Seven Joys of the Blessed Virgin soon spread over the entire Franciscan Order and became one of the favorite devotions of the friars.

Later it became customary to add two Hail Marys in honor of the seventy two years that Our Lady is said to have lived upon earth, and one Our Father and Hail Mary for the intentions of the Pope to gain the indulgences.

Indulgences

Members of the Three Orders of Saint Francis (including the Third Order Secular, Leo XIII, September 11, 1901), gain a plenary indulgence each time they recite the Franciscan Crown. No beads are necessary. This plenary indulgence can be applied to the souls in purgatory.

Indulgences Granted by Pius X

A. PLENARY INDULGENCES. The faithful gain:

I. A Plenary Indulgence for taking part in the public recital of the Crown in any church of the Three Orders of St. Francis.

2. A Plenary Indulgence if, after Confession and Communion (no other conditions), they recite the FRANCISCAN CROWN on the following feasts: Christmas (Dec. 25) ; Epiphany (Jan. 6) ; Sunday during the Octave of Epiphany; Easter; Immaculate Conception (Dec. 8); Annunciation (Mar. 25) ; Purification (Feb. 2) ; Visitation (July 2) ; Assumption (Aug. 15) ; Feast of the Seven Joys of the Bl., Virgin (Aug. 22) ; Nativity of the Bl. Virgin (Sept. 8).

3. A Plenary Indulgence once a month on any day after Confession and Communion, if they sax the FRANCISCAN CROWN every Saturday.

4. A Plenary Indulgence in the hour of death on the usual conditions if one has the rosary in his possession and has prayed it frequently.

B. PARTIAL INDULGENCES: The faithful can gain a Partial Indulgence of :

1. Seventy Years and Seventy Quarantines EVERY TIME they say the FRANCISCAN CROWN on any day of the week except Saturday.

2. One Hundred Years every time they say it on any Saturday of the year.

3. Two Hundred Years when they say it on the holydays of obligation.

4. Three Hundred Years when they say it on any feast of the Bl. Virgin not mentioned above for the Plenary Indulgences.

5. Ten Years for every good work they. perform for the honor of God or for the love of their neighbor, provided they carry the rosary about on their person and often recite it.

6. Ten Years every time they say seven Hail Marys in honor of the Seven Joys of the Bl. Virgin, provided they carry the rosary about on their person and often recite it.

NOTE: All these indulgences, except the one for the hour of death, can be applied to the poor Souls.

Manufactured by Amazon.ca
Bolton, ON

40650968R00020